THE ALL NEW STYLE OF MAGAZINE-BOOKS

INDIE FAITH
MAGAZINE

www.indiefaith.com

MP

MOCY PUBLISHING
WWW.MOCYPUBLISHING.COM

Printed by CreateSpace, An Amazon.com Company

GET INSPIRED BY THE #1 FAITH BASED MAGAZINE

INDIE FAITH
MAGAZINE

EDITOR-IN-CHIEF
D. Bailey and Courtney Benjamin
dbailey@indiefaith.com
cbenjamin@indiefaith.com

EDITORAL DIRECTOR
Sheree Cranford
sheree@indiefaith.com

GRAPHIC/WEB DESIGNER
D. Bailey
dbailey@indiefaith.com

ADVERTISEMENT MANAGER
Courtney Benjamin
advertise@indiefaith.com

ACCOUNT EXECUTIVE
Smart Office Cloud

PHOTOGRAPHERS
KaSiris Martez Xavier
Casino Bailey

CONTRIBUTORS
Anna Marie
Jimavis Arnold

COPY ORDERS & ADVERTISING OFFICE
Send Money Order or Check to:
Mocy Publishing
P.O. Box 35195
Detroit, Michigan 48235
(248) 812-9568
advertise@indiefaith.com

Copy Order Item #:
Indie Faith Magazine Issue #1 2016
S&H Plus Retail Price - $9.99 per copy

WWW.INDIEFAITH.COM
Printed by CreateSpace, An Amazon.com Company

MP
MOCY PUBLISHING

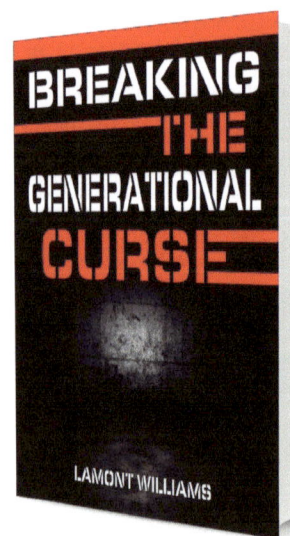

CONTENTS

12
FLYZON3
From gangster rap to now praising Christ with Gospel rap.

16
CHELLZZZ
A young soldier on fire for Jesus in concert and on tour.

20
CHRISTINA BENJAMIN
Gives you her heart with her new single and talks about her journey.

23
TOP 10 CHARTS
The hottest albums and digital singles this month features Marvin Sapp, Kirk Franklin, Ce Ce Winans, Tamala Mann, Mary Mary, and many more.

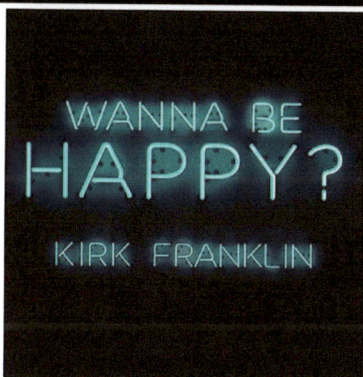

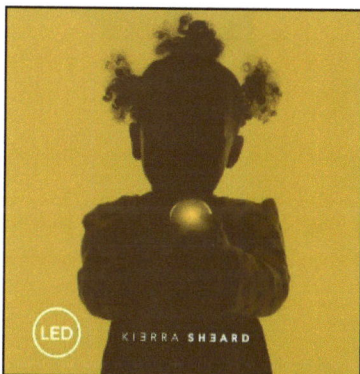

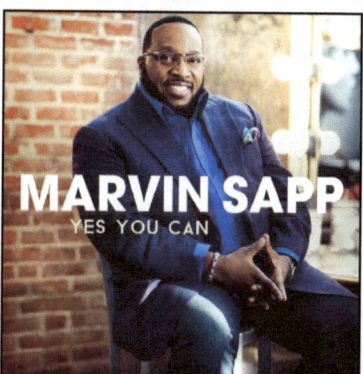

WANNA BE HAPPY?
KIRK FRANKLIN

LED
KIERRA SHEARD

MARVIN SAPP
YES YOU CAN

NEW ELECTRONICS

A LIST OF SOME OF THE PICK'S THIS MONTH.

BY JEFF WALKER

1 Samsung - 55" Smart 4K Ultra HD TV

Check out the Samsung 4K Ultra HD TV, the world's newest addition to PurColor Technology. The Samsung 4K Ultra HD TV also allows you to watch TV using the built-in Wi-Fi. You can stream music and download apps on the TV.

2 Apple TV

Get access to instant entertainment with the Apple TV. Just connect to the Internet and stream movies, listen to music, and access a wide variety of other content. You can also connect your iPhone or iPad to the Apple TV for streaming more apps.

3 WowWee - MiP Robot

The WowWee MiP 0825 robot is a robot that plays games, drives, dances, battles, balances, responds to motions. This is all controlled remotely controlled by a compatible iOS or Android cell phone for ease of use. The dual wheels allow smooth, simple mobility.

4 LG - ChromeBase 21.5" All-In-One - Intel Celeron

This LG ChromeBase 22CV241-W all-in-one computer features built-in wireless networking and a 1.3MP webcam, which makes it simple to chat with family and friends over the Internet. The Intel® Celeron® processor is reliable for everyday computing.

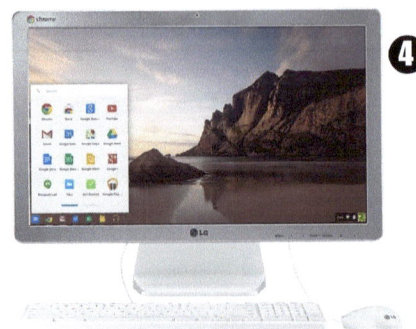

The biggest thing to happen to iPhone since iPhone.

iPhone 6s

A Real Living Testimony

TERESA CREGGETT-MOORE GIVES US HER TRUE TESTIMONY ON HOW HER LIFE WAS HEADED FOR SELF-DESTRUCTION.

by Teresa Creggett-Moore

I remember being drunk many nights; not from alcohol but, from a life filled with negativity, sin, self-pity, and internal rage. My journey during my drunken binges left me throwing up confusion, anger, hate, betrayal, and falling into the unconscious pool of self-destruction. Sometimes the girl staring at me in the mirror looked like a stranger. I could not remember who she was; those almond slanted sad eyes seemed familiar.

I was taught to pray as a child; believing in what was naked to the eye was hard for me to grasp. I did it without understanding and it was a way of life passed down from strong women. I remember drifting off the narrow road from fear of the unknown; speeding towards the broad road of destruction. I pushed everyone who cared authentically away and clung tightly to people who didn't care about my life one way or another.

I remember driving without a license to drive; no map to give me direction for my destination. I just wanted to be free and travel uncharted territories. It did not matter who my driver was or where we were going; I was satisfied with just being a passenger until one day we made a wrong turn. It was as if we were driving in a never ending circle; a voice was clear, loud, direct, and unfamiliar. It told me to get off the road and return home.

I was next to death living and dying in my right mind; no longer confused or suffocating from the grasp of negativity, I regurgitated negativity, sinful ways, ignorant thoughts, destructive actions. I no longer wanted to be me and free in this life. I remember running towards the narrow road through the storms of life and flood filled nights. I remember falling to my knees and surrendering from fear of being out of GOD's will.

I am a quiet soul living in a violent world with many testimonies to reach people like myself who are or once had a problem with being who they were designed to be in this lifetime. My life is not my own; I owe it to GOD and his divine will be done according to his favor over my life. I am just a woman who is a passenger in this vehicle and my driver is GOD.

I am not perfect. I am not holier than thou. I am not preaching to you, I am speaking to your spirit. I am not sinless and have been sinful. I am a masterpiece created by our Father in heaven just like you. I am a living testimony and I hope you can relate to my thoughts.

Teresa Creggett-Moore

I will live for GOD until the day he calls my name to return home. I am unashamed to call upon GOD; I am surrendering to GOD and him alone. There is none greater than him. Ask GOD to forgive your transgressions and release you into a secret garden to refine who you are written to be in this life.

There are no two people alike. Therefore, I will dance in the wind like stars in the sky, smile at strangers bright like the sun. I will remember by brokenness when I want to share my living testimonies. It is living proof your love is unconditional and your forever with us on this journey called life.

A Powerful Message from God

ANNA MARIE MCCUTCHEN GIVES GOD THE GLORY AFTER HER LIFE WAS TURNED AROUND FROM A MESS TO A MESSAGE.

by Anthony Ambrogio

From a Mess To a Message is both a memoir and a self-help book. Gospel singer Anna Marie McCutchen provides examples from her life and appropriately selected scriptural quotations to illustrate that sometimes the mess IS the message.

She shows how even our darkest days have a purpose unto God and that, if you let go and let God lead you, your life can have purpose and meaning. Readers can use her text to make a message out of what they mistakenly believe is the mess of their lives.

You can find more books & music from Anna Marie McCutchen on her website: www.annamariegospel.com

From a Mess to a Message
By Anna Marie McCutchen.

Available from Amazon.com and other online stores

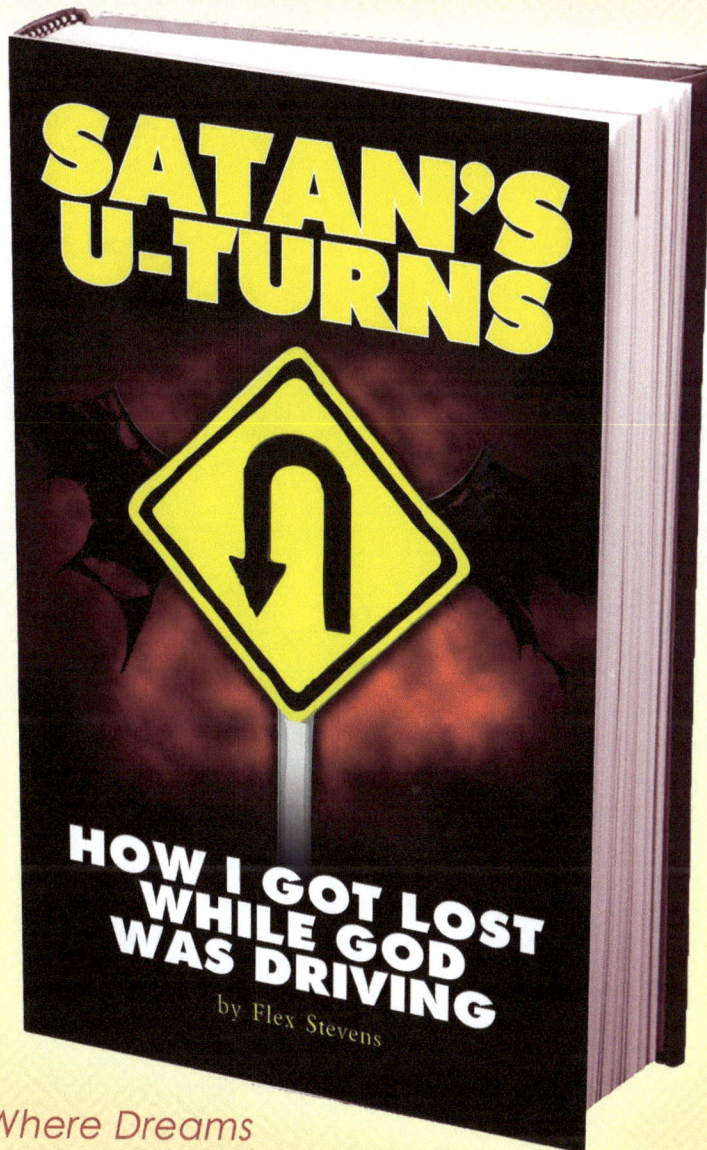

This Duo is Supa Dupa Fly

FROM GANGSTA RAP TO GOSPEL RAP THE DUO FLYZON3 TAKES FLIGHT WITH ALL NEW MUSIC FROM THEIR NEW ALBUM.

by Cheraee C.

The Lyons' on Fox 2 don't have anything on the divine Detroit Holy Hip Hop Husband and Wife duo Flyzon3, which entails Derrick and Denise Lyons'. The group Flyzon3 is a pseudonym for Forever Loving Yahweh, and the three symbolizes the trinity (the Father, the Son, and the Holy Ghost.) The Dynamic Duo (who's better known as Waderboy and Wadergurl) style is holy, but hood. In life, it's a struggle to get people to praise God obediently, but their approach inspires people from all walks of life to praise God.

Both Derrick and Denise have come from difficult pasts and gangster rap music backgrounds. God wanted to take the two through some trials and tribulations so they could be a true testimony to others. Through church and salvation, the dynamic duo retorted their rap backgrounds to Holy Hip Hop. They taught each other how to love again and utilize music as an outlet to express their innermost feelings, their experiences, and their faith in God.

In July 2015, they released their debut album "Supa fly." The album includes two blazing hot singles which are "Send Me" and "Fresh." Both singles have amazing videos you should check out on YouTube. Before the album, they released the EP "Supa fly" in March 2013.

This year Flyzon3 received three nominations at the Rhythm of Gospel Awards in Birmingham, Alabama. They won two awards which include the Holy Hip Hop Artist of the Year and the Holy Hip Hop Song of the Year. The duo has hosted many events and featured on the Darinda Clark Show, the Greg Davis show. WRTV, and many others. Also, in 2015, the duo has founded their own record label which is God Mafia Records and the CEO of that is Maurice L. Hardwick. The label has two artists signed which are Dre Beeze and Convictor.

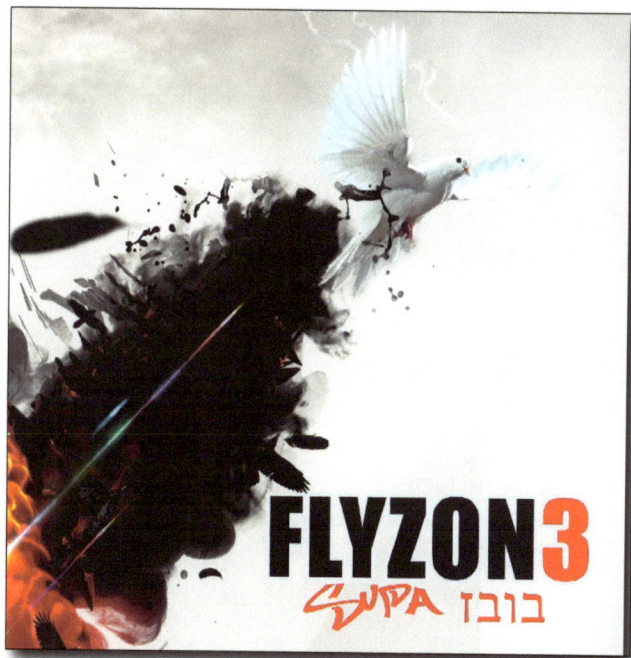

Flyzon3's music is available on YouTube, Spotify. CDXtreme, Itunes, etc. You can follow them on Instagram and Twitter @flyzon3 and on Facebook @ Flyzon3 Musiq. To stay posted to their movement please visit their website at flyzon3.bandcamp.com.

Pastor Marvin Sapp's Journey

WHILE ON THE JOURNEY FOR CHRIST PASTOR MARVIN SAPP GIVES A BLESSING TO THE WORLD WITH HIS SONG "YES YOU CAN".

by Anna Marie

Marvin Sapp, a world renown gospel singer and preacher, is one who has persevered through many hard trials. The loss of his wife has been one of the hardest to cope with namely. He continues to travel the country with his ministry.

An anointed man of God who pours out passionately with preaching the gospel and also more expressive through singing. Pastor Sapp is from Detroit. He currently pastors a church in Grand Rapids called Lighthouse Full Life Center. His latest single is entitled "Yes You Can". This song is sweeping the nation and has a massive impact on almost everyone who has a strong faith in God and refuses to give up.

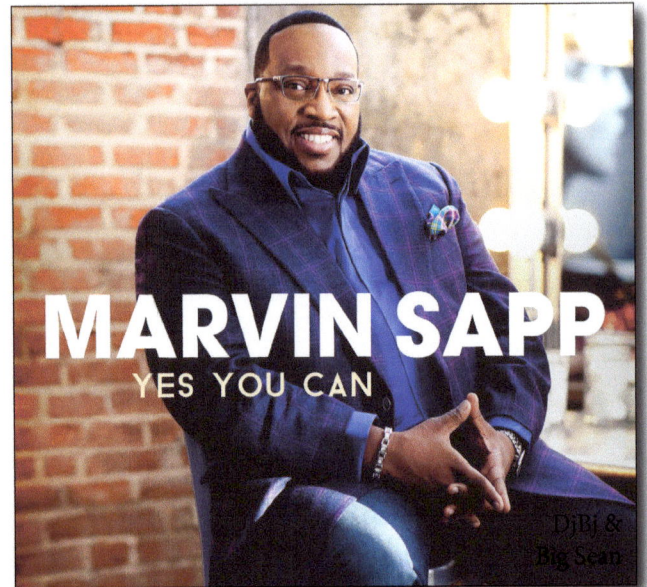

MARVIN SAPP
YES YOU CAN

INDEPENDENT CHRISTIAN LABEL / ENTERTAINMENT COMPANY

BENJAMIN ENTERTAINMENT GROUP

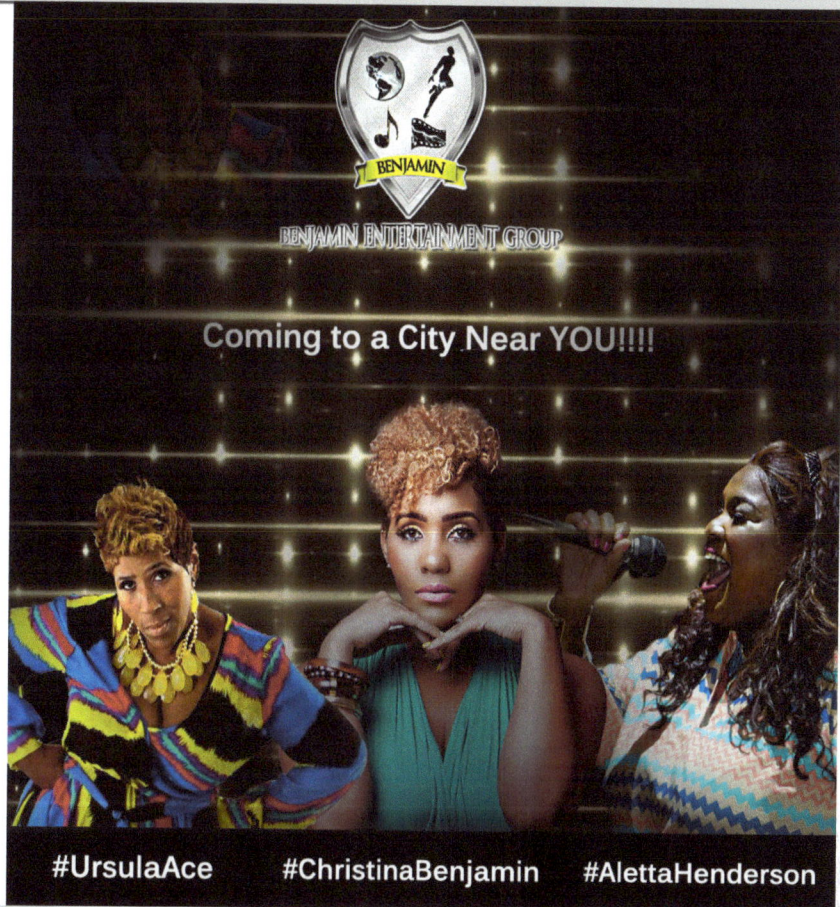

Coming to a City Near YOU!!!!

#UrsulaAce   #ChristinaBenjamin   #AlettaHenderson

SERVICES

-CD DUPLICATIONS

-ARTIST DEVELOPMENT

-WEBSITES

-DISTRIBUTION

ALBUMS

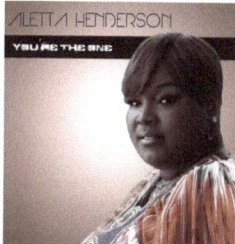

WWW.BENJAMINENTGROUP.COM

f BENJAMINENTGROUP

Detroit's Gospel Prodigy

CHELLZZZ IS UPLIFTING THE YOUTH AND HAS ONE OF THE BEST GOSPEL ALBUMS IN THE COUNTRY AND ONLINE.

Photography by Anna Marie

With seven years in the gospel zone is Detroit's gospel prodigy Chellzzz. Chellzzz is a Hip Hop singer and rapper who composes and produces his own music. Chellzzz's style is glorious, his beats are modish, and his songs are enriching. Chellzzz is an unsigned artist, but he has worked with a handful of upcoming Detroit artists from his genre of music. Some of those gospel artists include Disciple and M3.

Chellzzz has released many projects uplifting the community with his version of gospel music. Chellzzz's latest single is titled "The Impossible" which was released early October 2015. His most recent project is titled "The Holy Tape" which was released in the beginning of 2015. Some of his other projects include "No Filters," and "True

Disciple." Chellzzz's music is currently available on iTunes, YouTube, and www.band camp.com. In 2016, Chellzzz is definitely going to keep redefining himself as an artist, and broadening his career to bigger and better opportunities. He will also be releasing a new mixtape at the first quarter of the year.

You can follow Chellzzz on Facebook @Chellz Robinson and like his artist page @Chellzzz. You can follow him on IG @kingdom_chellzzz, and follow his YouTube channel @Kingdom Chellzzz. For the latest on Chellzzz you can join his holy movement and visit his website www.chellzmusic.com.

STYLES BY CHRISTINA

"BE BEAUTIFUL BE YOU"

CUSTOM WIG UNITS

JACKY CLARK CHISHOLM   ALEXIS SPIGHT   DORINDA CLARK-COLE

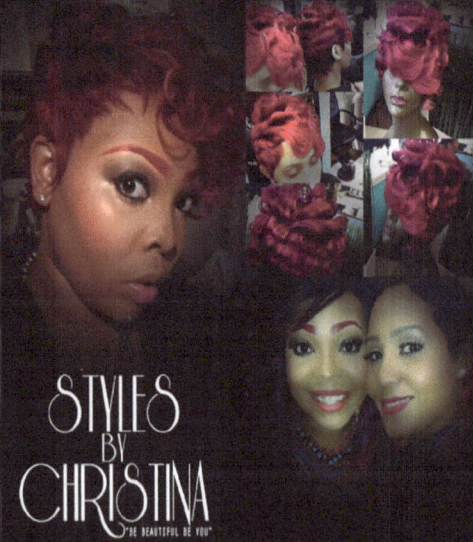

STYLESBYCHRISTINA

STYLESBYCHRISTINA82

WWW.STYLESBYCHRISTINA.COM

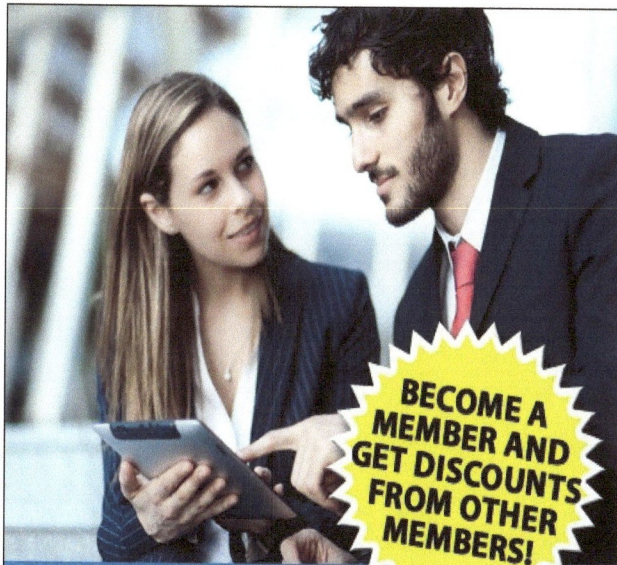
Spotify News

INDIE ARTIST PERRIN LAMB EARNS OVER $56,000 FROM ONE SONG ON SPOTIFY WITHOUT A RECORD DEAL.

by Semaja Turner

Perrin Lamb is an indie singer-songwriter from Nashville. He's been in music for over a decade. Never signed to a record or publishing deal. He decided to distribute his music through CD Baby, which an indie music distributor that distributes for independent artists.

In January of 2014, a song that Perrin wrote called "Everyone's Got Something" was selected to feature on the Your Favorite Coffeehouse playlist on Spotify by their editorial team. At this time, Perrin's song had been out for about a year and wasn't doing that well in the industry. It wasn't until the song hit the playlist and boom. The song went from hundreds to millions of plays in no time.

As of today, the song has gained about 13 million streams worldwide. Perrin's was paid for getting over 10,929,203 streams from Spotify for his song "Everyone's Got Something". From that, he earned a total of $40,131.55 (which was left after CD Baby's 9% distribution fee.) Perrin also earned mechanicals and digital performance royalties that make up the remainder of the total $56,000.

Finding Joy on Her Journey

CHRISTINA BENJAMIN IS SPEADING PRAISE ACROSS THE WORLD WITH HER BRAND NEW SONG FOR CHRIST "GIVE ME YOUR HEART".

by Cheraee C.

An international gospel virtuoso on the rise is Detroit's finest Christina Benjamin. She is a celebrity hair stylist, an actress, a model, a Christian recording artist, and a song-writer. Presently, Christina is an independent artist signed to Benjamin Ent Group. Devoted to fine arts, Christina attended a fine arts school and began performing in stage plays which led her on the path of music.

Her latest single is titled "Give Me Your Heart." In 2011, she released her first astounding EP titled "Pieces of Me" which features her first single "Breathe." She has also featured on a few compilation albums including Releasing A Sound, Rhythm of Gospel, and The Black Project and worked with many local gospel artists. Her music is available on iTunes, Spotify, Google Play, YouTube, and all digital download stores. Also, her music is available in God's World and Lifeway Christian Stores.

Christina has achieved much prestige in all avenues of her career thus far. In 2012, Christina won the Rhythm of Gospel Award and the American Heart Association Award. Just recently in October of 2015, she opened up for Grammy-winning Chrisette Michelle at the Detroit Music

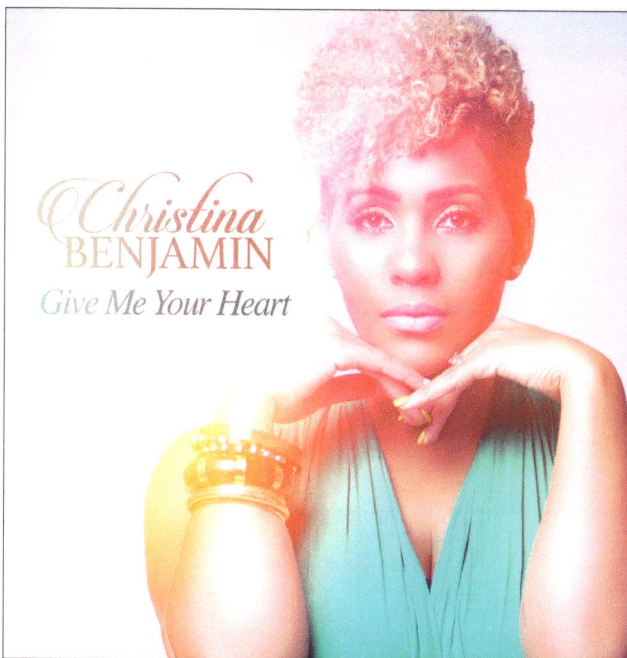

Hall. She has traveled the world from the U.S. to overseas showcasing her talent. Some events she has performed at including the Rhythm of Gospel Showcase and the Dorinda Clark Show. She has performed in plays with big names including Clifton Powell, Carl Payne, Sisqo, Shirley Murdock, Peggy James, and Eric Deon.

In 2016, Christina is in pursuit to release her first album, arranging her first concert, and planning a promotional tour. To stay linked to Christina's movement you can visit her website at www.christinabenjamin.com. You can also follow her on Facebook @Christina Benjamin and Instagram @stylesbychristina82.

GET INSPIRED BY THE FAITH BASED MAGAZINE

INDIE FAITH

MAGAZINE

PLUS
ANNA MARIE
URSULA ACE
TOP 10
GOSPEL
SONGS

ALL NEW

Flyzon3

ALL NEW ALBUM
"SUPER F.L.Y" IS
CREATING A
HUGE BUZZ ON
SOCIAL MEDIA
& ONLINE

Christina Benjamin

GIVES YOU HER
HEART ON HER
NEW HIT SINGLE
AND TALKS ABOUT
HER JOURNEY

Chellzzz

CHRISTIAN RAPPER
HAS POWERFUL
WORDS TO SAY

US - $9.99

01 >

9 770317 847001

JANUARY 2016 No.1
WWW.INDIEFAITH.COM/MAGAZINE

ORDER YOUR ISSUE FOR $9.99
Issue 1 - Christina Benjamin: Item #IFMVOL1
Send money order plus $3.95 S&H to: Mocy Publishing, LLC
P.O. 35195 * Detroit, MI 48235

TOP 10 CHARTS

TOP 10 DIGITAL SINGLES AND ALBUMS
JANUARY 1, 2016

TOP 10 CHARTS

MARVIN SAPP - BLESSING THE WORLD WITH HIS HIT SINGLE.

TOP 10 SINGLES CHART OF THE MONTH

No.	Artist - Song Title
1	MARVIN SAPP - YES YOU CAN
2	CANTON JONES - FILL ME UP AGAIN
3	MARY MARY - GO GET IT
4	LE'ANDRIA JOHNSON - SOONER OR LATER
5	TAMELA MANN - I CAN ONLY IMAGINE
6	CE CE WINANS - WE WELCOME YOU (HOLY FATHER)
7	SHIRLEY CAESAR - WHEN YOU PRAY GOD ANSWERS
8	ALEXIS SPIGHT - ALL THE GLORY
9	ANNA MARIE - MY TESTIMONY
10	ALETTA HENDERSON - YOU'RE THE ONE

TOP 10 ALBUMS CHART OF THE MONTH

No.	Artist - Album Title
1	CE CE WINANS - THY KINGDOM COME
2	KIERRA SHEARD - LED (EP)
3	DETROIT VOL. 1 - RELEASING A SOUND
4	KIRK FRANKLIN - WANNA BE HAPPY?
5	TAMELA MANN - BEST DAYS
6	LE'ANDRIA JOHNSON - THE AWAKENING OF LE'ANDRIA JOHNSON
7	MARY MARY - GO GET IT
8	SHIRLEY CAESAR - GOOD GOD
9	URSULA ACE - TRUST
10	DEITRICK HADDON - MASTERPIECE

Good God

ARTIST: Shirley Caesar
REVIEWER: Cheraee C.

Shirley Caesar, a well-respected legend is both a singer and preacher. She has many awards and achievements. Her "Good God" record is just one of her most outstanding albums that have blessed us all. I have had the privilege of enjoying her in concert. This iconic artist travels the world spreading the gospel and making a positive impact on all age groups.

Shirley is also known as the queen of gospel music. As she continues to touch the lives of many, may the Lord keep her well with divine protection. Thank you, Pastor Shirley Caesar for sharing your preaching and singing with us all.

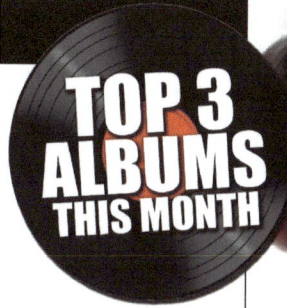

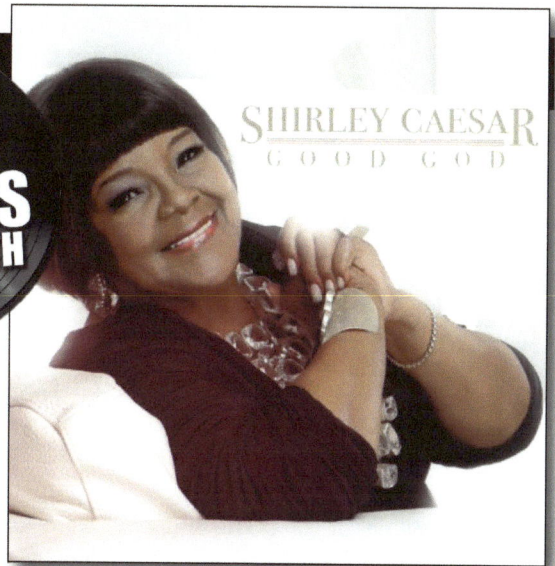

TOP 3 ALBUMS THIS MONTH

SHIRLEY CAESAR
GOOD GOD

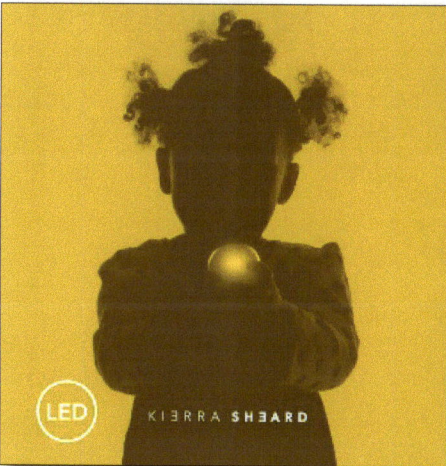

LED - EP

ARTIST: Kierra Sheard
REVIEWER: Jason White

Kierra Sheard is one of the wittiest musical artists for her age bracket to bring such contemporary style music combined with her anointing. Thank God for her style of music that she brings to our young generation. Thanks for blessing us with your music.

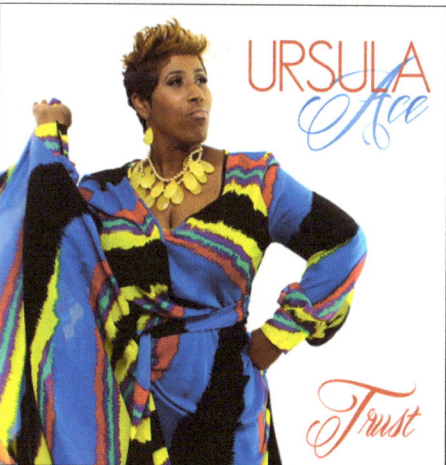

LED   KIERRA SHEARD

Trust - EP

ARTIST: Ursula Ace
REVIEWER: Suzy Stafford

Praised for her ability to usher in the spirit of worship, Ursula Ace is an exceptional praise and worship singer who certainly believes in allowing the Spirit of the Lord to use her to HIS glory. Her new EP 'Trust' is a great sound and a masterpiece God would approve of.

URSULA Ace
Trust

Walking by Faith in Prosperity

HOW WALKING BY FAITH LEADS TO THE PATH OF PROSPERITY FOR ANNA MARIE WITH HER NEW BLESSING FROM CHRIST .

by Cheraee C.

A strong-willed woman adamant about spreading her testimony by any means is the Detroit native Anna Marie. For over 15 years Anna Marie has been involved with gospel music. Now she is spreading her testimony through more than just music and praise dance. She is influencing people through literature including books and magazines and theatre.

Anna Marie is an ambitious gospel artist on a mission. Some of her albums include, Aim High, Jesus is Coming Holiday album, and Just Believe. Each one of her albums is inspirational and reaches out to all generations, and people from all walks of life, Anna's music is available on YouTube, Soundcloud and her website (annamariegospel.com). She also has an audio and paperback book available titled "From A Mess To A Message."

Anna released her debut book "From A Mess To A Message" in December 2011 through G Publishing. From A Mess To A Message is both a memoir and a self-help book that entails how a mess can be a message. A couple of years later she went back to the drawing board and released another book through G Publishing. This book is titled "Aim High Journal" and is a motivational novel that helps build on success through God's faith. Both of her books are available online on Amazon and Barnes&Noble.

After publishing two books, Anna Marie published a gospel magazine. The Anna Marie Faith Magazine was released December 2015 and is available online on Amazon. This magazine is a representation of everything that is gospel locally and nationally. It's a place where commendable people in the community can promote their businesses and give personal accounts of their testimonies of how God has impacted their life.

You can visit her website at www.annamariegospel.com, and you can follow her on Facebook @Anna McCutchen. With an unstoppable drive and purpose, Anna Marie has many more gospel ventures underway.

The Sweet Sound of Music

URSULA ACE IS AN UPCOMING GOSPEL SENSATION WITH A VOICE THAT WILL HAVE YOU SHOUTING FOR JOY AND PRAISE.

by Cheraee C.

An independent artist slowly, but surely rising into the gospel world is Detroit's own Ursula Ace. Nicknamed the "Psalmstress," Ursula has a solid church background and was always inspired by gospel music. A lot of the Music she composes comes from chapters and scriptures that are correlated with the Book of Psalms.

Currently signed to the Benjamin Entertainment Group, the future holds many things for Ursula. Just recently on 12/13/15, Ursula released her first EP titled "Trust." Some amazing songs from her EP include "Trust" and "I'm Blessed." On New Year's Day of 2016, Ursula's music will be available on iTunes, Spotify, Google Play, and Lifeway Christian Store.

In 2016, Ursula plans to expand herself and her gospel career. She plans to release an album, bring forth media like videos to highlight her songs, and go as far as she can go in the gospel industry. It's no doubt she will be on YouTube, Soundcloud, television, radio, and on the road spreading her love for the gospel. She is humble and definitely ready for the challenge.

To stay connected with Ursula and her gospel movement, you can follow her on Facebook @Ursula Thepsalmstress Ace, and on Instagram @psalmstress_sing.

NEXT 2 GLOW

SUDANA FOWLER THE MOUTH PEACE FOR JESUS.

After writing music all of my life, I finally received the name Mouth Peace from God in 2012. It was after I decided to take music ministry serious. I asked God, and he told me this is who I am. When it comes to ministry, music, spoken word, etc. I am an Oracle for God. I was led by the Holy Spirit to branch off and do ministry through clothing design.

The term God gave me is apparel evangelism. It's an opportunity to witness through clothing. Therefore combining graphic designs and T-Shirt printing, it became MPFORJ custom apparel and design. I create and provide design services for others.

There are numerous other things that I do in God's kingdom including preaching the gospel, prison ministry, poetry, and writing children's books. To contact me go to www.mpforj.com My fan page is Mouthpeace and Instagram is mouthpeace4Jesus

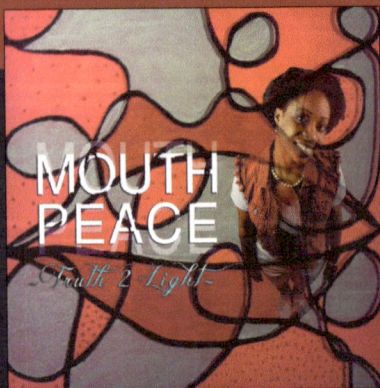

Mouth Peace - Truth 2 Light
(Mouth Peace for Jesus)

From the Streets to Salvation

HOW LAWRENCE E. JOHNSON FOUND HIMSELF IN TROUBLE WHILE DEALING WITH THE DEVIL BUT HE SURRENDER AND GOT SAVED.

by Lawrence E. Johnson

Lawrence Edward Johnson II was born April 7, 1973, on Detroit's westside. He grew up with his three sisters and a young nephew in a single parent home where his mother worked two full-time jobs to make ends meet. Growing up impoverished, in a household that lacked little to no adult supervision, Lawrence soon found himself caught up in the street life that lures so many young men to the drug scene. "I saw guys my age with all the cash and the fresh gear and I said to myself, "I want a piece of that. I was recruited by some of the older cats in the hood who got me started selling crack. It was all good till I started to get jammed up every time I turned around."

"Back in the 80's, the system was more lenient on younger offenders. I had a rap sheet a mile long with every kind of offense: drug possession, weapon possession, endangerment, recklessness, etc. I beat every one, but then I got caught with 350 grams of cocaine. I was charged with drug possession with intent to distribute and deliver which carried a max of 25 years. Frankly, I don't know how I beat those charges..... but at that time, I had applied to my current position at Cobo Hall. When I got called into the interview, the manager asked me about the charges on my clearance. I told him to what I believe to this day is what Jesus had to me to tell him. I said, "Sir, I know I have charges on my clearance, but please take into consideration that those charges say "pending" next to them, not "guilty." In January 2016, I'll have 20 years at Cobo Hall.

After being acquitted on all charges, I started to move away from that lifestyle. I still wasn't living right, but God's grace was upon me. I had side-stepped any prison time or felonies on my record. What was amazing is that in all of it, I was attending church faithfully with my mother. She was the one committed to the church; I was just committed to getting her there and back. I was still drinking, smoking weed, getting high, and running the streets. I hadn't yet had a personal relationship with Jesus Christ though I was faithfully in the church every Sunday with Mama. I just thank God for my mother's prayers that covered me."

SNAP SHOTS

Email Your Snap Shots to
snapshots@indiefaith.com

A Divine Floral Shop

DESIGNING AMAZING FLORAL ARRANGEMENTS FOR ALL OCCASIONS ON THE EAST SIDE OF DETROIT.

by Cheraee C.

Kozy Floral is a trendy flower shop located on the east side of Detroit, Michigan at 14945 Harper Avenue. Kozy specializes in floral designs for all occasions especially weddings and birthdays.

If you are interested in floral arrangements for any occasion, you can contact Robert Jones at (313) 333-9275 or Facebook him @Robert Jones.

THE ALL NEW STYLE OF MAGAZINE-BOOKS

INDIE FAITH

MAGAZINE